EASY PIANO CD PLAY-ALONG

Volume 24

Orchestrated arrangements with you as the soloist!

LENNON & McCARTNEY
FAVORITES

ISBN 978-1-4234-6721-2

HAL•LEONARD® CORPORATION
7777 W. BLUEMOUND RD. P.O. BOX 13819 MILWAUKEE, WI 53213

Visit Hal Leonard Online at
www.halleonard.com

CONTENTS

ACROSS THE UNIVERSE

Words and Music by JOHN LENNON
and PAUL McCARTNEY

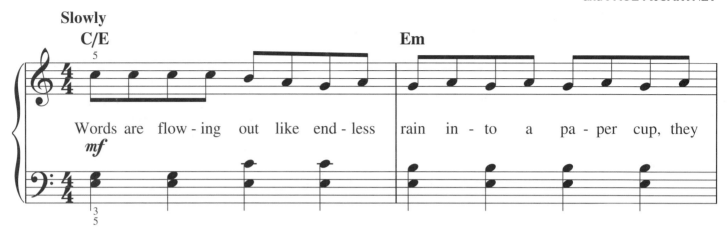

Words are flow-ing out like end-less rain in-to a pa-per cup, they

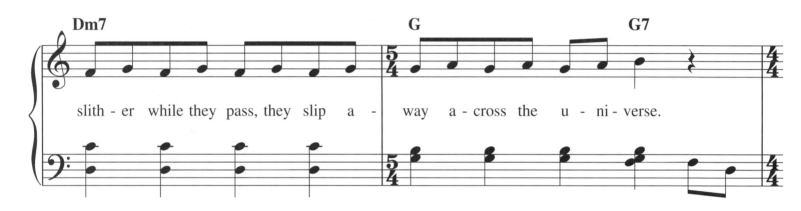

slith-er while they pass, they slip a-way a-cross the u-ni-verse.

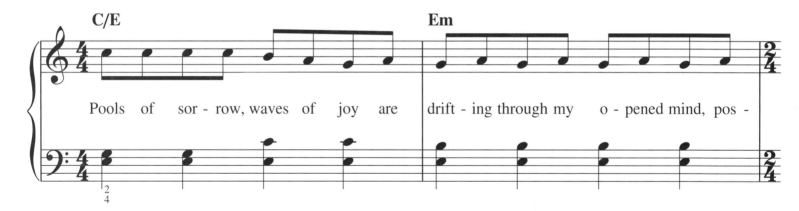

Pools of sor-row, waves of joy are drift-ing through my o-pened mind, pos-

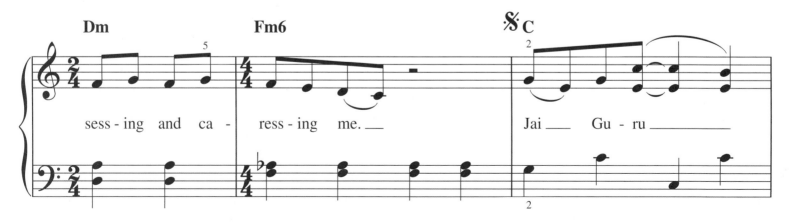

sess-ing and ca-ress-ing me. ___ Jai ___ Gu-ru ___

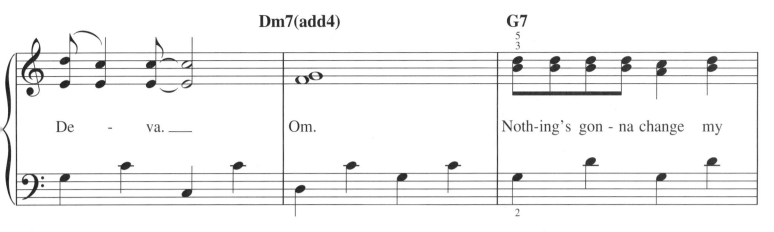

Dm7(add4) — De - va. ___ Om.

G7 — Noth-ing's gon - na change my

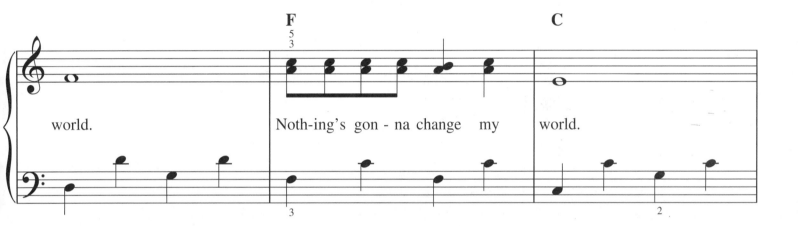

world.

F — Noth-ing's gon - na change my

C — world.

G7 — Noth-ing's gon - na change my

world.

F — Noth-ing's gon - na change my

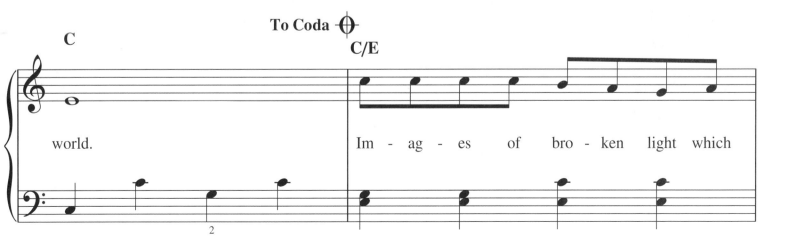

C — world.

To Coda ⊕

C/E — Im - ag - es of bro - ken light which

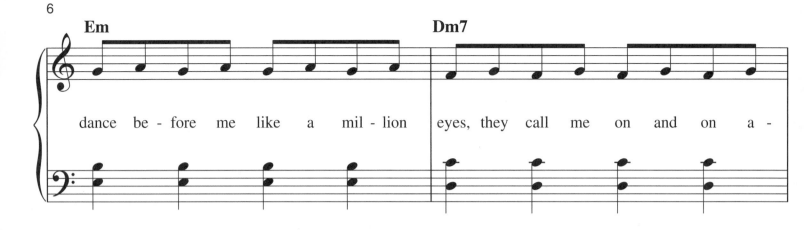

Em ... **Dm7**

dance be - fore me like a mil - lion eyes, they call me on and on a -

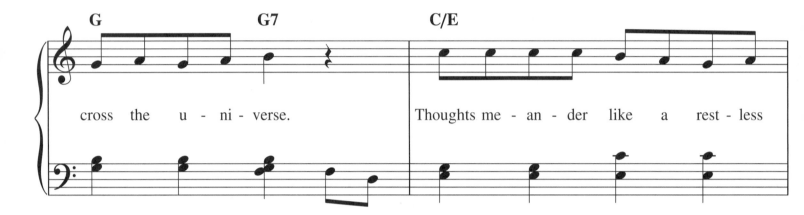

G ... **G7** ... **C/E**

cross the u - ni - verse. Thoughts me - an - der like a rest - less

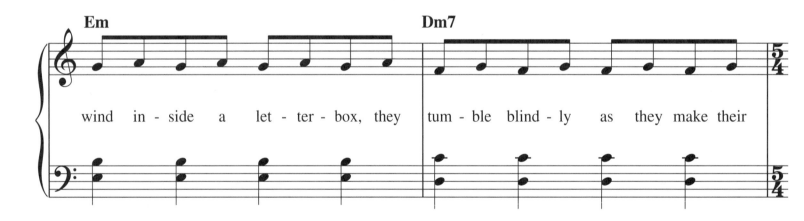

Em ... **Dm7**

wind in - side a let - ter - box, they tum - ble blind - ly as they make their

D.S. al Coda

G ... **G7**

way a-cross the u - ni - verse.

CODA

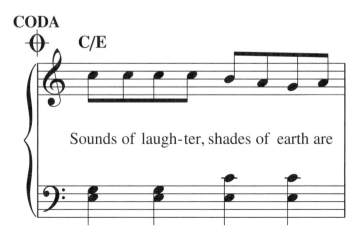

C/E

Sounds of laugh-ter, shades of earth are

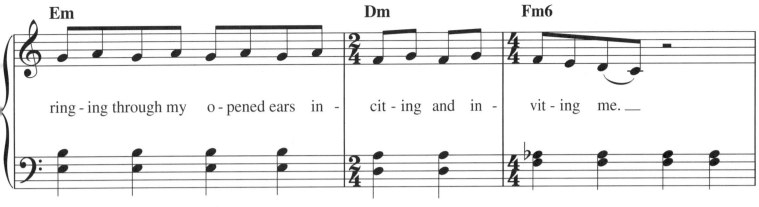

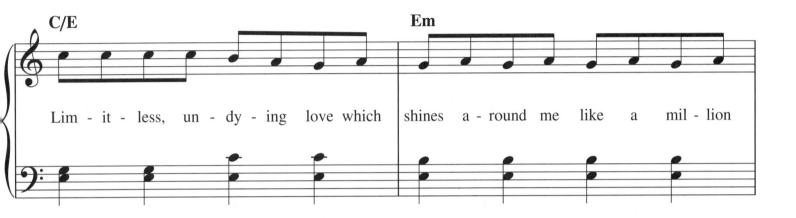

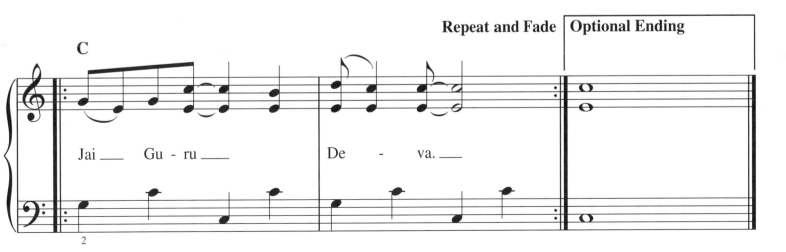

ALL YOU NEED IS LOVE

Words and Music by JOHN LENNON
and PAUL McCARTNEY

Moderately, not too fast

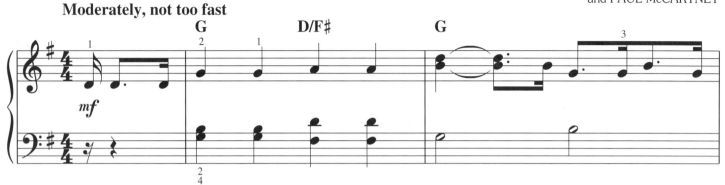

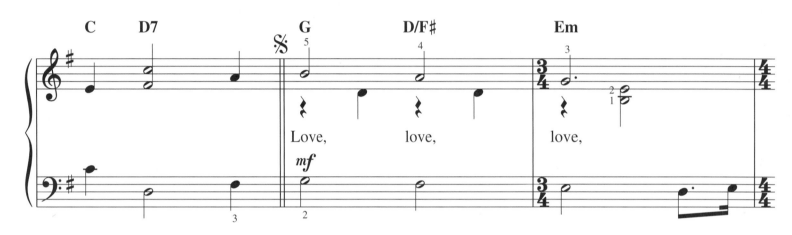

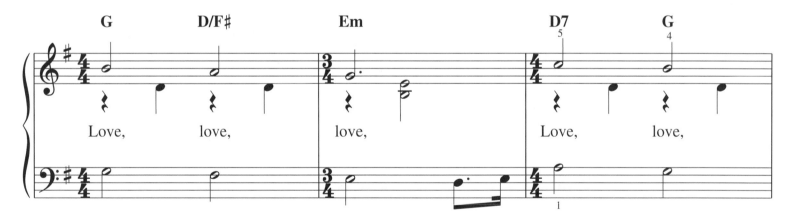

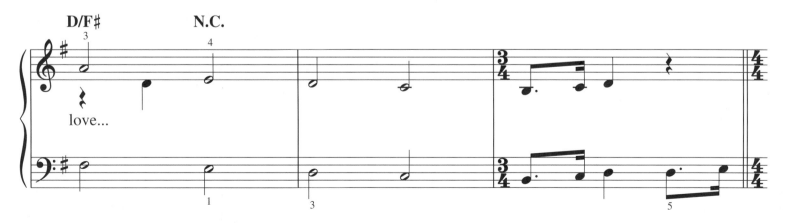

There's noth-ing you can do that can't be done.
Noth-ing you can make that can't be made.
Noth-ing you can know that is-n't known.

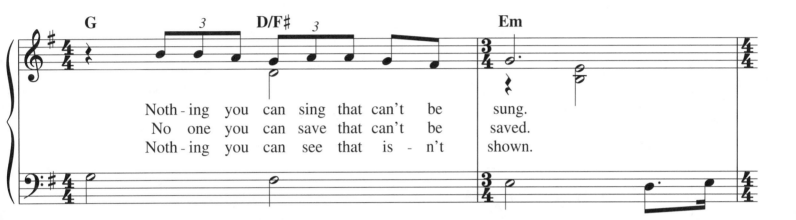

Noth-ing you can sing that can't be sung.
No one you can save that can't be saved.
Noth-ing you can see that is-n't shown.

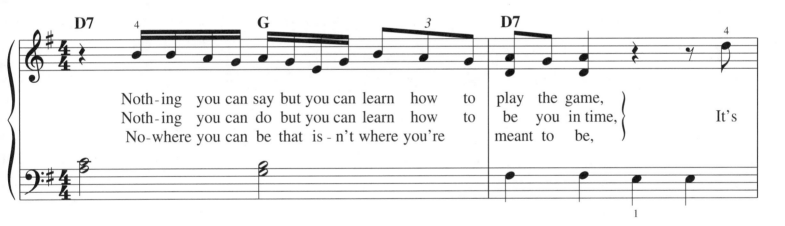

Noth-ing you can say but you can learn how to play the game,
Noth-ing you can do but you can learn how to be you in time,
No-where you can be that is-n't where you're meant to be,

It's

eas - y:

1.
N.C.

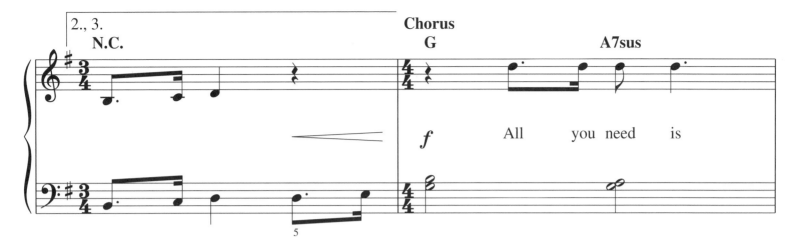

AND I LOVE HER

Words and Music by JOHN LENNON
and PAUL McCARTNEY

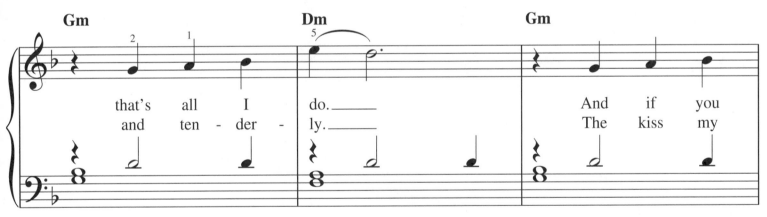

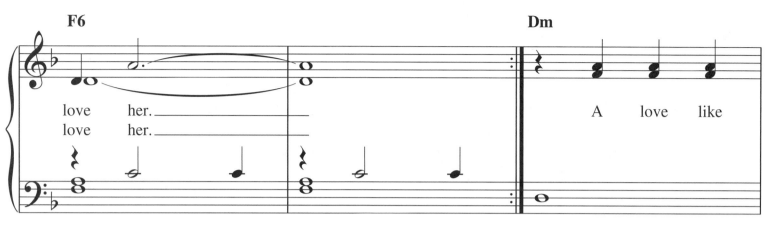

love her._____
love her._____

A love like

ours

could nev - er die

as long as

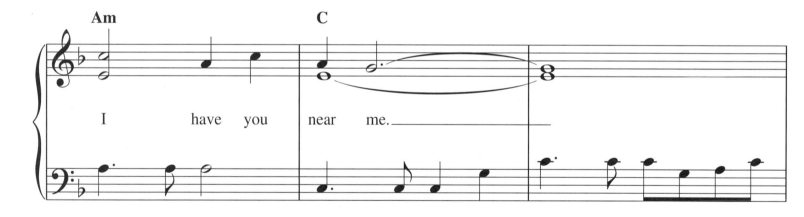

I have you near me._____

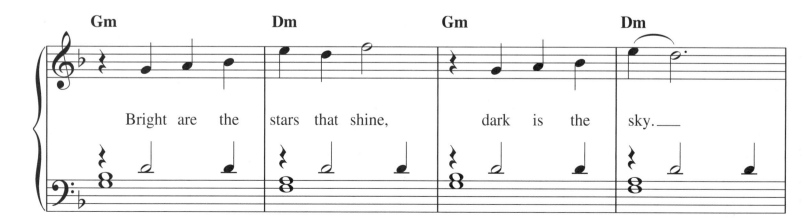

Bright are the stars that shine, dark is the sky.___

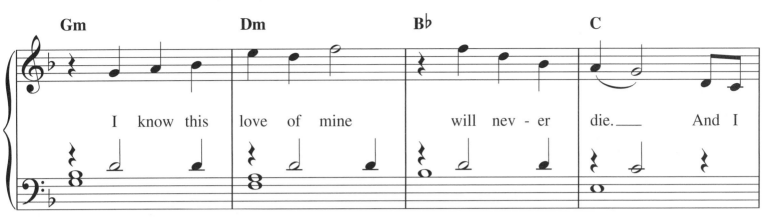

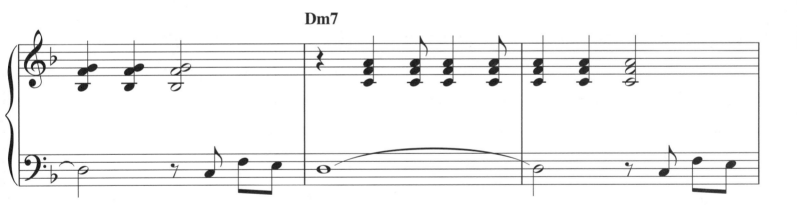

HELLO, GOODBYE

Words and Music by JOHN LENNON
and PAUL McCARTNEY

Not too fast

You say   yes, __   I say   no, __   you say   stop, __   and

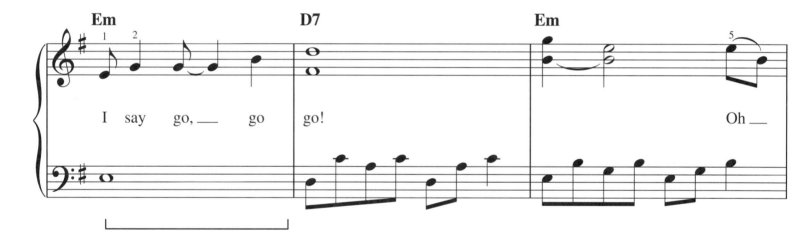

I say   go, __   go   go!   Oh __

no,   you say good-bye   and   I   say hel-

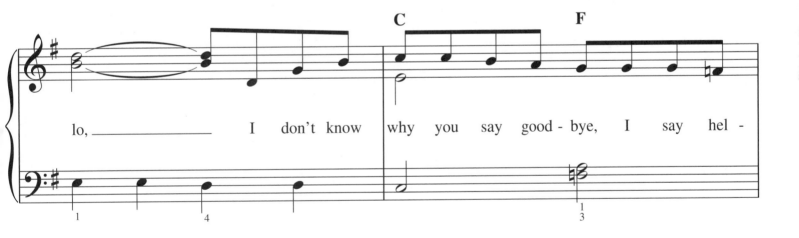

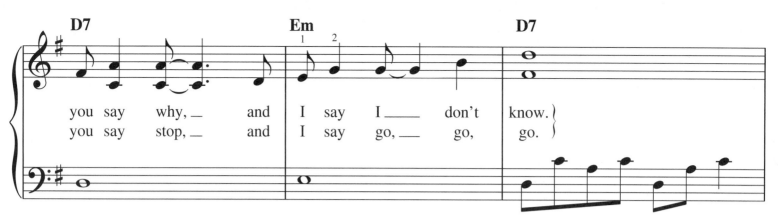

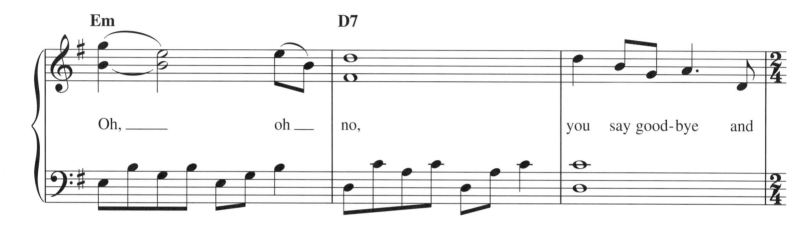

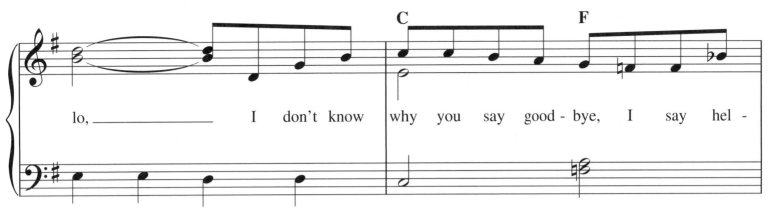

lo, _____ I don't know why you say good-bye, I say hel-

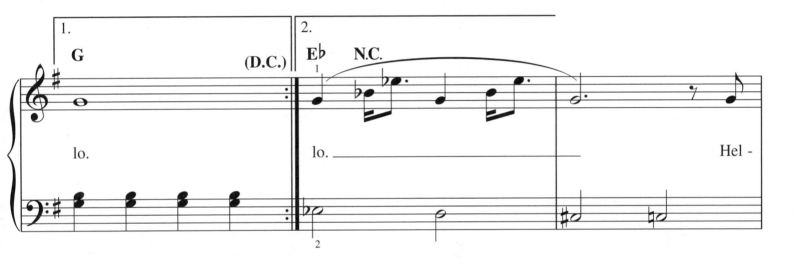

lo. lo. _____ Hel-

lo. _____ Hel - lo, _____ he - ba ___ hel -

lo - a...

I WANT TO HOLD YOUR HAND

Words and Music by JOHN LENNON
and PAUL McCARTNEY

With a steady Rock beat

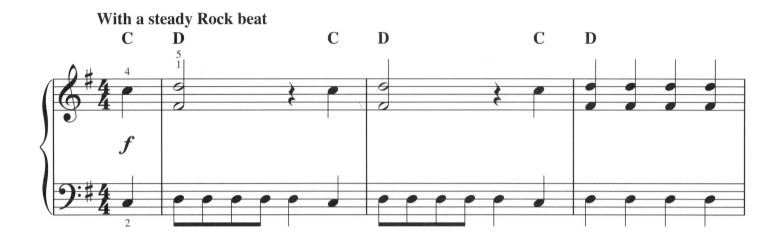

Oh yeah, I'll _____ tell you some - thing
please ____ say to me _____

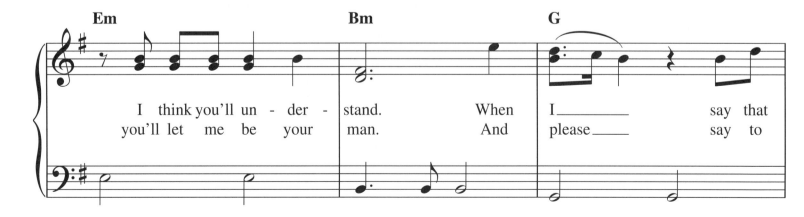

I think you'll un - der - stand. When
you'll let me be your man. And

I _____ say that
please ____ say to

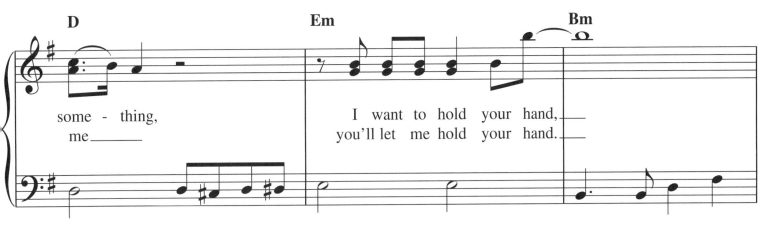

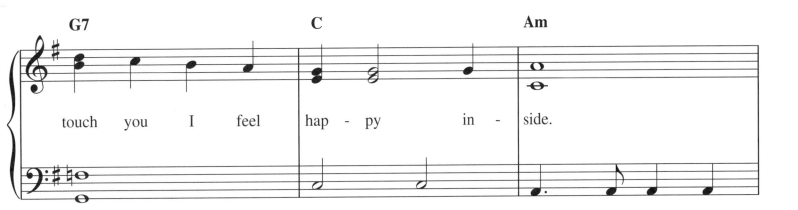

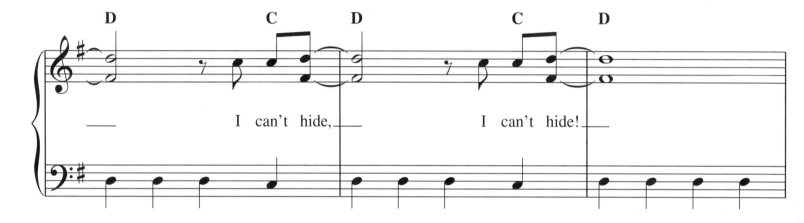

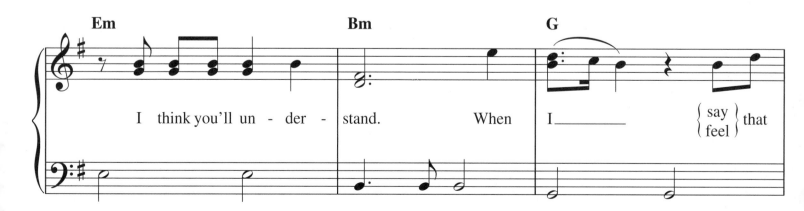

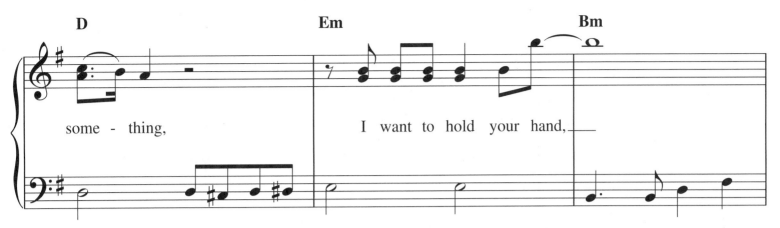

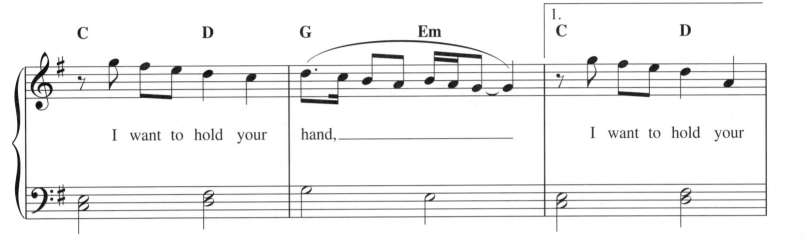

IF I FELL

Words and Music by JOHN LENNON
and PAUL McCARTNEY

Moderately slow, but not dragging

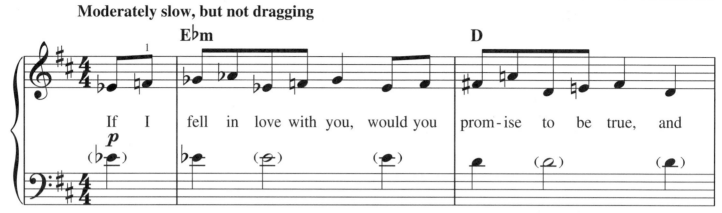

If I fell in love with you, would you prom-ise to be true, and

help me un-der-stand? 'Cause I've been in love be-fore, and I

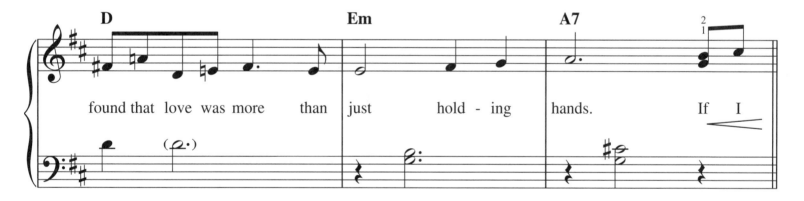

found that love was more than just hold-ing hands. If I

give my heart to you, I
trust in you, oh please, don't

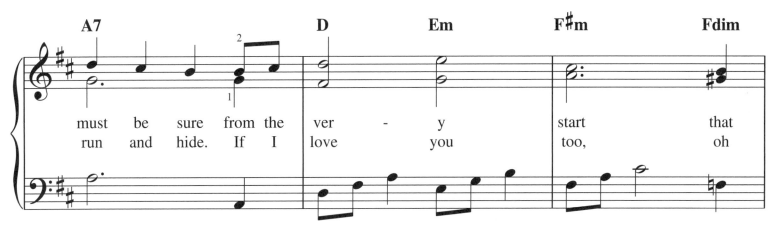

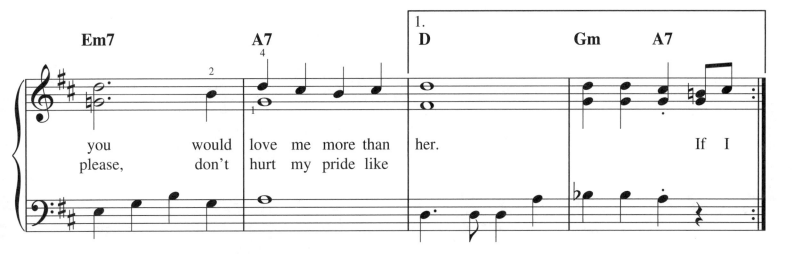

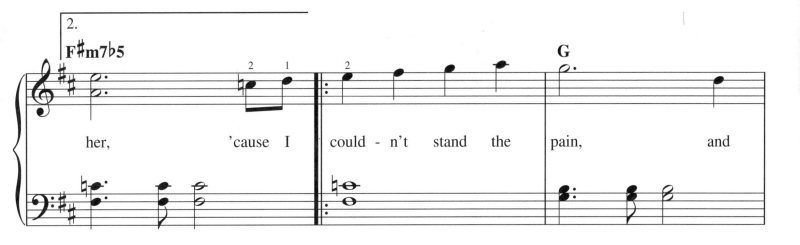

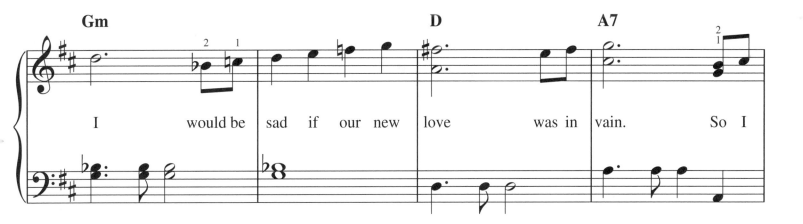

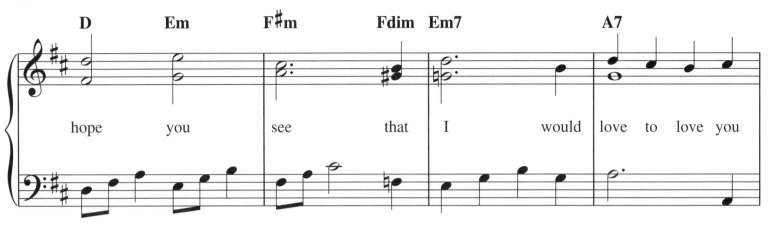

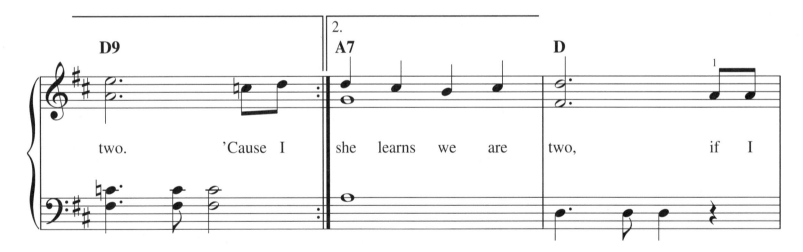

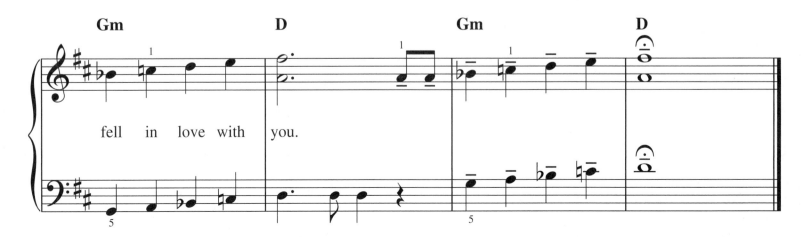

MICHELLE

Words and Music by JOHN LENNON
and PAUL McCARTNEY

Gentle Ballad (but not too slow)

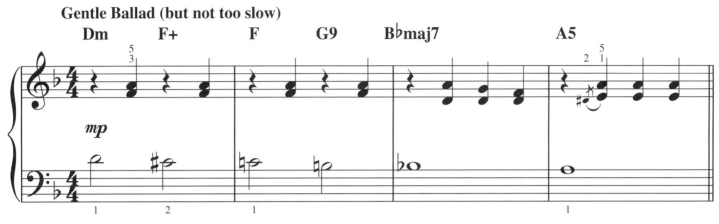

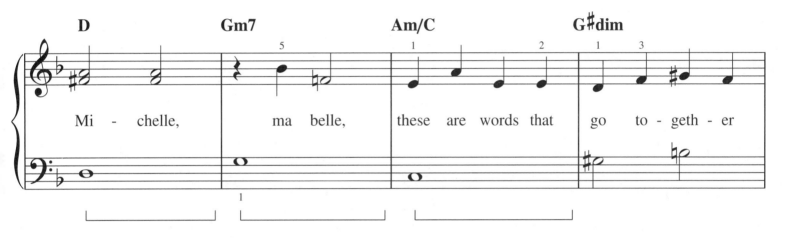

Mi - chelle, ma belle, these are words that go to - geth - er

well, my Mi - chelle.

Mi - chelle,
Mi - chelle,
I love you...

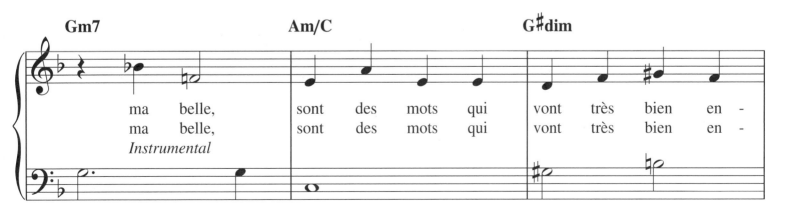

ma belle,
ma belle, sont des mots qui vont très bien en -
Instrumental sont des mots qui vont très bien en -

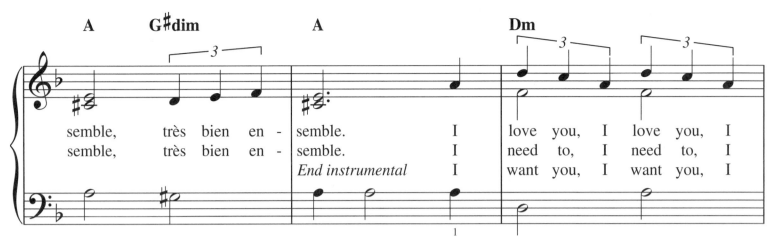

semble,	très bien en -	semble. I
semble,	très bien en -	semble. I
		End instrumental I

love you, I love you, I
need to, I need to, I
want you, I want you, I

love you,	that's all I want to	say
need to,	I need to make you	see
want you,	I think you know by	now,

un - til I find a	way, _____ I will	say the on - ly
oh, what you mean to	me. _____ Un -	til I do I'm
I'll get to you some -	how. _____ Un -	til I do I'm

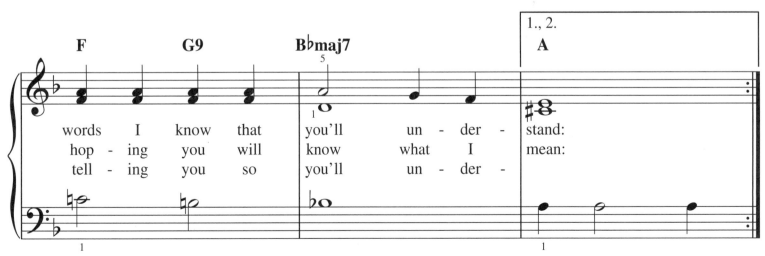

		1., 2.
words I know that	you'll un - der -	stand:
hop - ing you will	know what I	mean:
tell - ing you so	you'll un - der -	

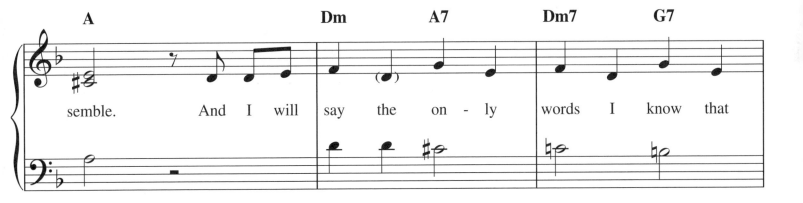

LET IT BE

Words and Music by JOHN LENNON
and PAUL McCARTNEY

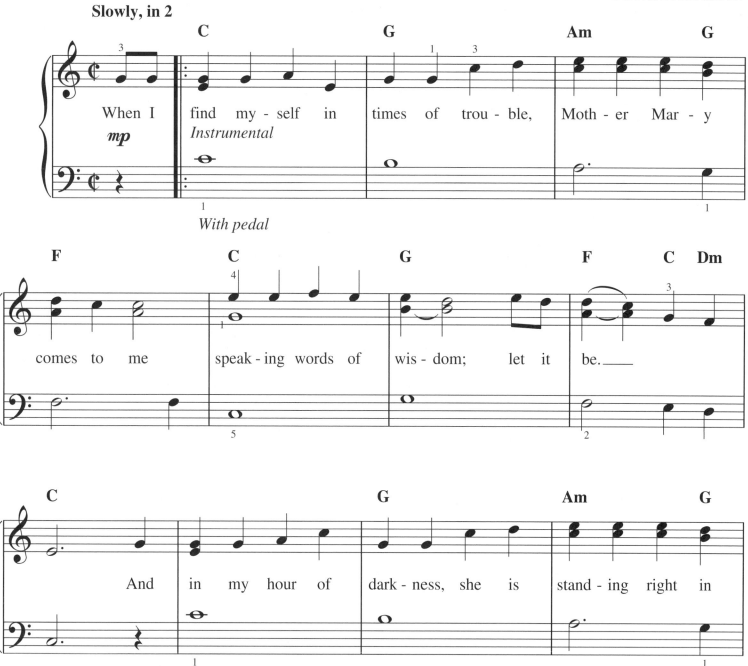

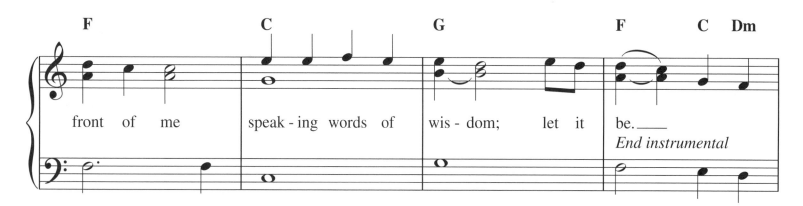

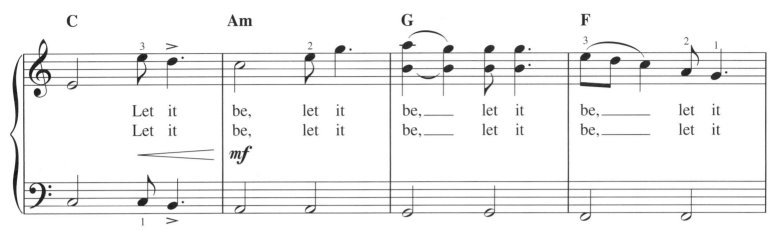

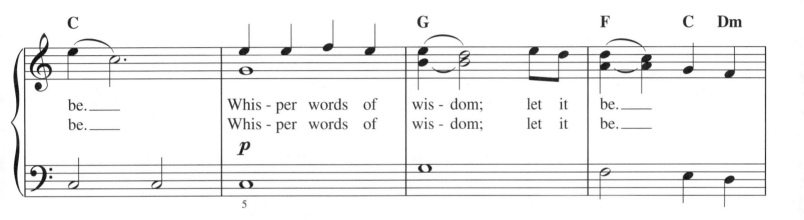

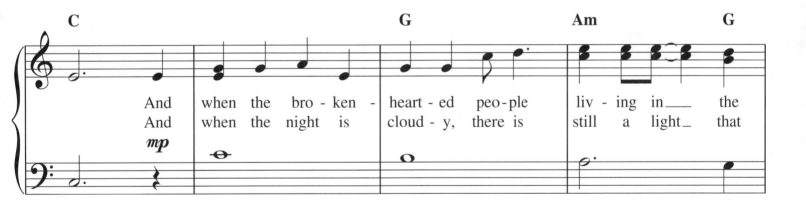

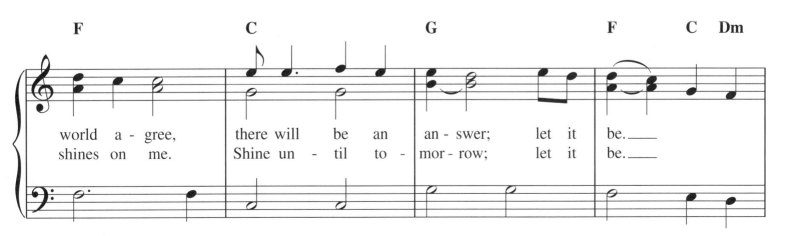

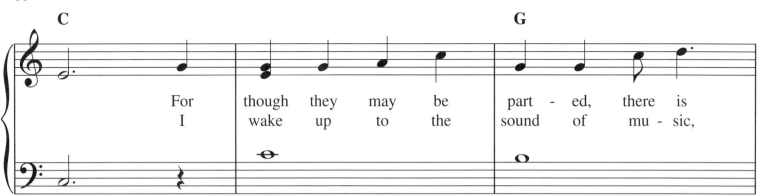

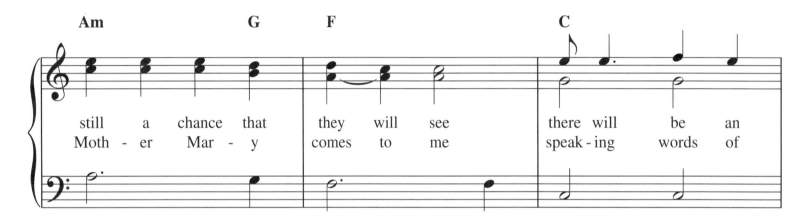

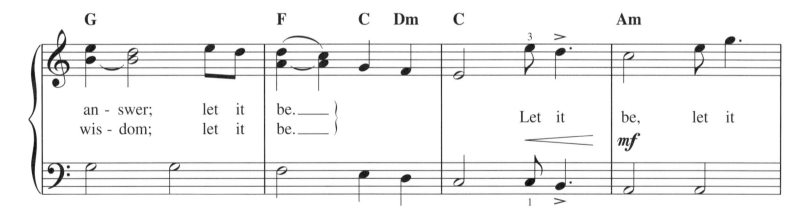

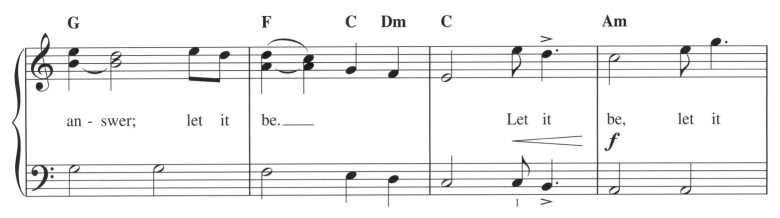

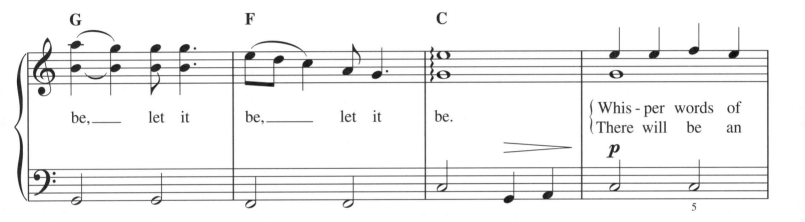

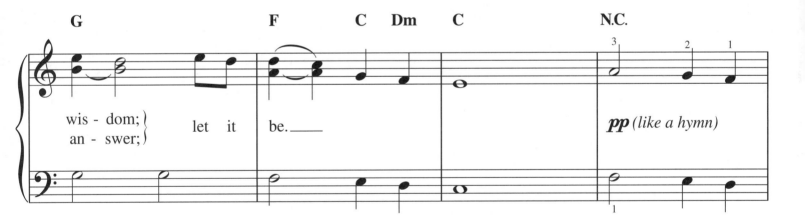

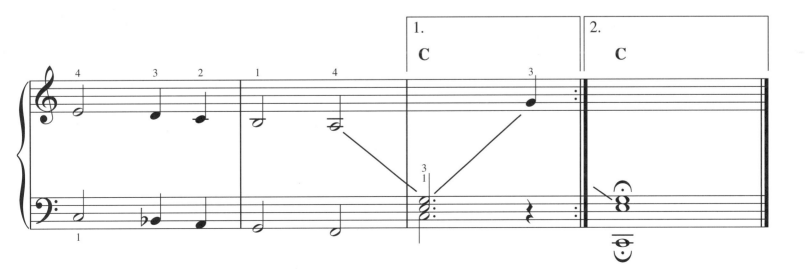

PENNY LANE

Words and Music by JOHN LENNON
and PAUL McCARTNEY

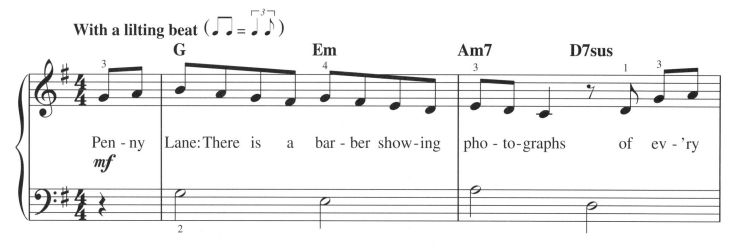

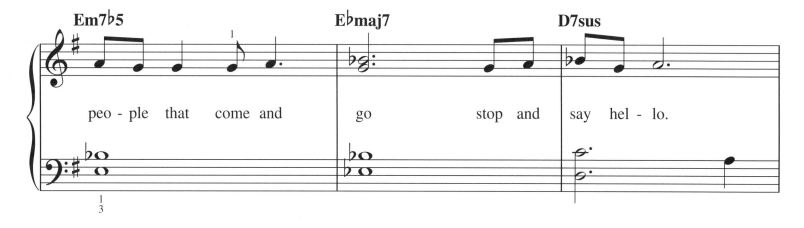

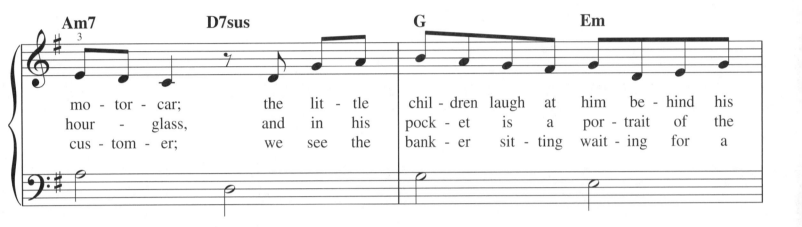

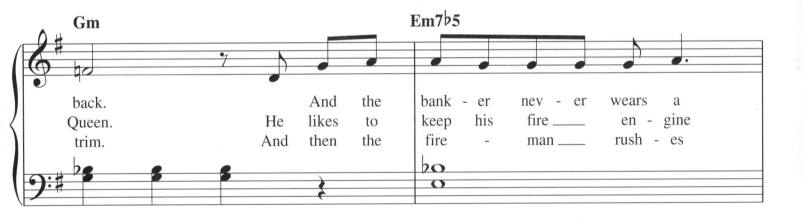

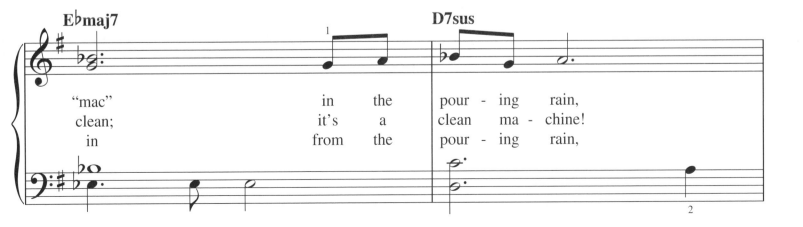

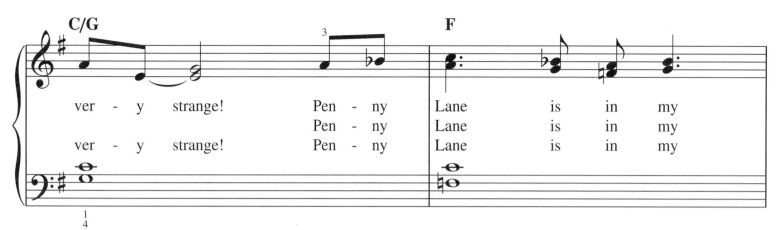

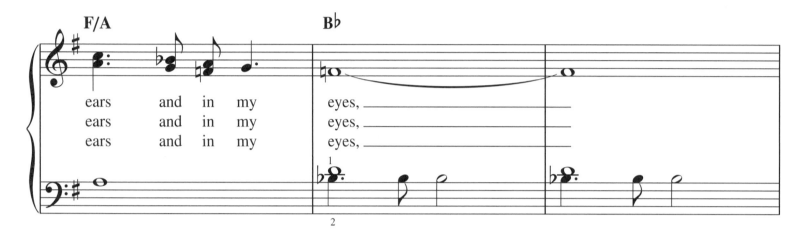

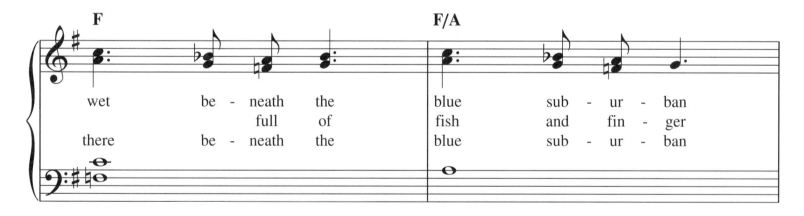

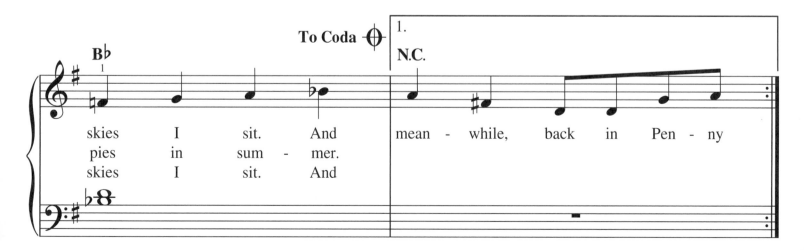

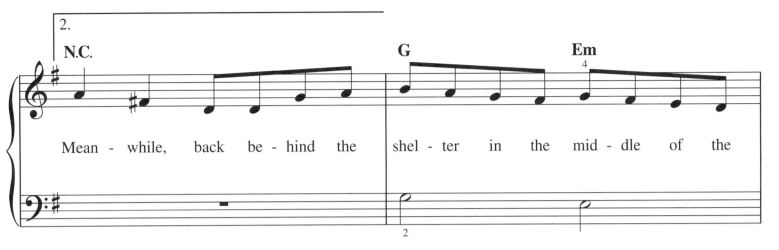

Meanwhile, back behind the shelter in the middle of the

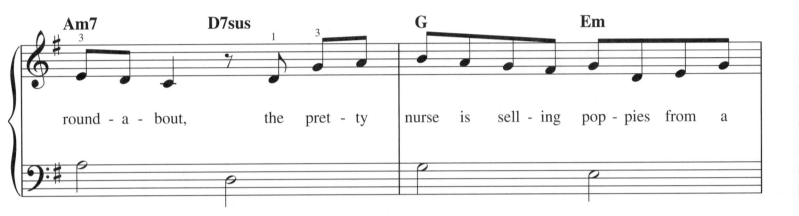

roundabout, the pretty nurse is selling poppies from a

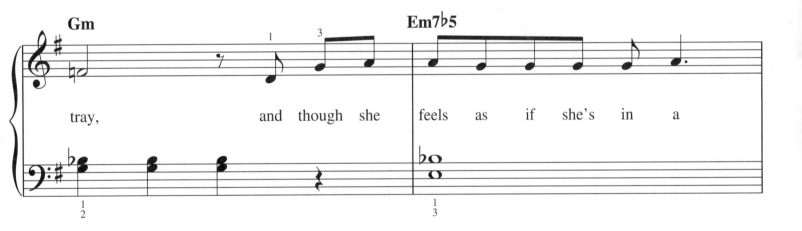

tray, and though she feels as if she's in a

play, she is anyway.

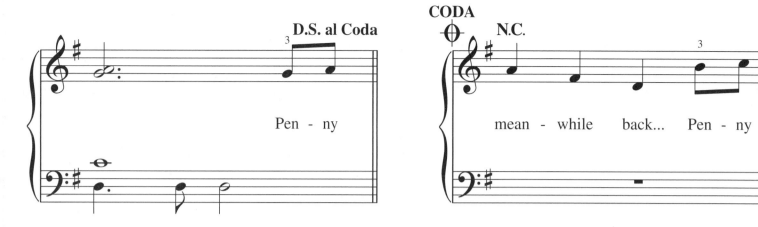

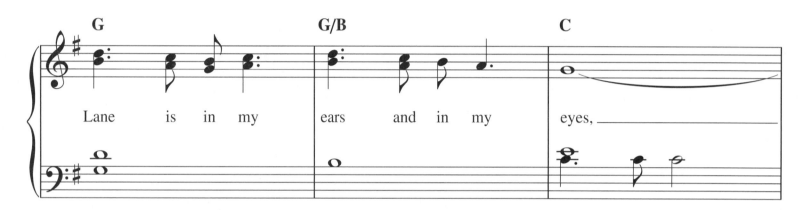

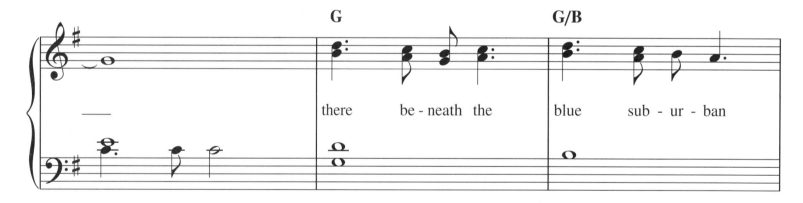

YELLOW SUBMARINE

Words and Music by JOHN LENNON
and PAUL McCARTNEY

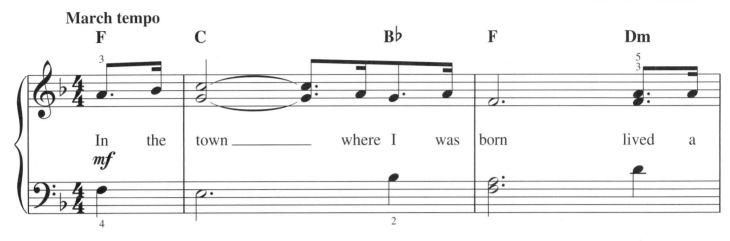

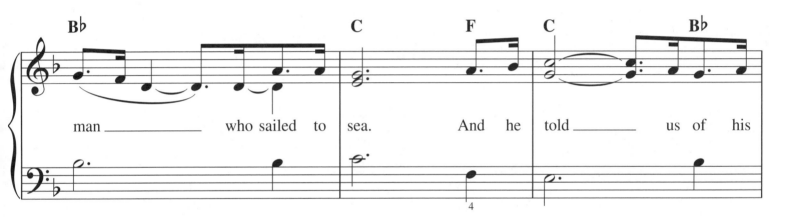

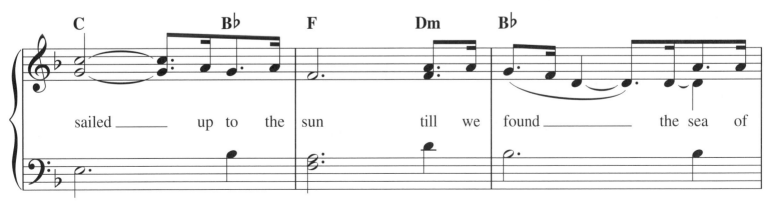

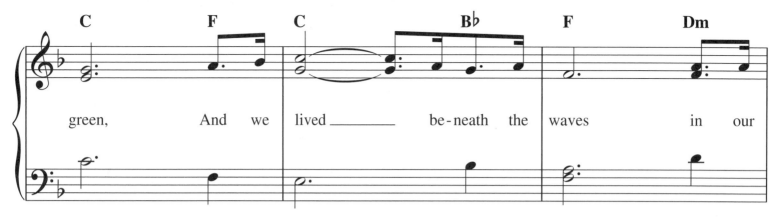

C   **F**   **C**   **B♭**   **F**   **Dm**

green,   And we lived _____ be-neath the waves in our

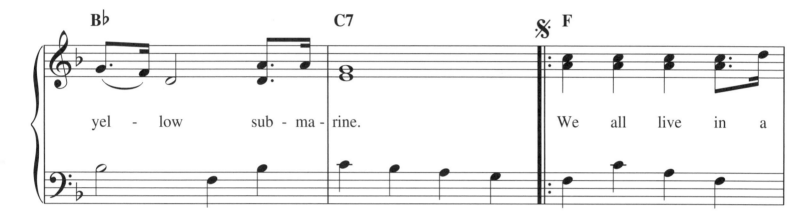

B♭   **C7**   **F**

yel - low sub - ma - rine.   We all live in a

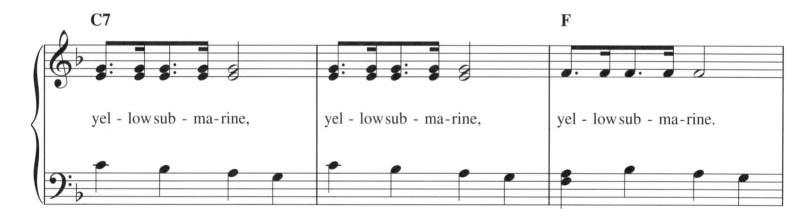

C7   **F**

yel - low sub - ma - rine,   yel - low sub - ma - rine,   yel - low sub - ma - rine.

C7

We all live in a   yel - low sub - ma - rine,   yel - low sub - ma - rine,

yel - low sub - ma - rine.

{ And our friends _____ are all on board, man - y

As we live _____ a life of ease, ev - 'ry

mf

more of them _____ live next door. And the band _____ be - gins to

one of us _____ has all we need. Sky of blue _____ and sea of

1.

play:

2.

D.S. al Fine

green in our yel - low sub - ma - rine.

EASY PIANO CD PLAY-ALONGS

Orchestrated arrangements with you as the soloist!

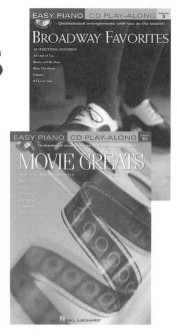

This series lets you play along with great accompaniments to songs you know and love! Each book comes with a CD of complete professional performances and includes matching custom arrangements in Easy Piano format. With these books you can: Listen to complete professional performances of each of the songs; Play the Easy Piano arrangements along with the performances; Sing along with the recordings; Play the Easy Piano arrangements as solos, without the CD.

GREAT JAZZ STANDARDS – VOLUME 1
Bewitched • Don't Get Around Much Anymore • How Deep Is the Ocean • It Might As Well Be Spring • My Funny Valentine • Satin Doll • Stardust • and more.
00310916 Easy Piano $14.95

FAVORITE CLASSICAL THEMES – VOLUME 2
Bach: Air on the G String • Beethoven: Symphony No. 5, Excerpt • Gounod: Ave Maria • Grieg: Morning • Handel: Hallelujah Chorus • Pachelbel: Canon • Tchaikovsky: Waltz of the Flowers • and more.
00310921 Easy Piano $14.95

BROADWAY FAVORITES – VOLUME 3
All I Ask of You • Beauty and the Beast • Bring Him Home • Cabaret • Close Every Door • I've Never Been in Love Before • If I Loved You • Memory • My Favorite Things • Some Enchanted Evening.
00310915 Easy Piano $14.95

ADULT CONTEMPORARY HITS – VOLUME 4
Amazed • Angel • Breathe • I Don't Want to Wait • I Hope You Dance • I Will Remember You • I'll Be • It's Your Love • The Power of Love • You'll Be in My Heart.
00310919 Easy Piano $14.95

HIT POP/ROCK BALLADS – VOLUME 5
Don't Let the Sun Go Down on Me • From a Distance • I Can't Make You Love Me • I'll Be There • Imagine • In My Room • Rainy Days and Mondays • Total Eclipse of the Heart • and more.
00310917 Easy Piano $14.95

LOVE SONG FAVORITES – VOLUME 6
Fields of Gold • I Honestly Love You • If • Lady in Red • More Than Words • Save the Best for Last • Three Times a Lady • Up Where We Belong • We've Only Just Begun • You Are So Beautiful.
00310918 Easy Piano $14.95

O HOLY NIGHT – VOLUME 7
Angels We Have Heard on High • God Rest Ye Merry, Gentlemen • It Came upon the Midnight Clear • O Holy Silent Night • What Child Is This? • and more.
00310920 Easy Piano $14.95

A CHRISTIAN WEDDING – VOLUME 8
Cherish the Treasure • Commitment Song • How Beautiful • I Will Be Here • In This Very Room • The Lord's Prayer • Love Will Be Our Home • Parent's Prayer • This Is the Day • The Wedding.
00311104 Easy Piano $14.95

COUNTRY BALLADS – VOLUME 9
Always on My Mind • Could I Have This Dance • Crazy • Crying • Forever and Ever, Amen • He Stopped Loving Her Today • I Can Love You Like That • The Keeper of the Stars • Release Me • When You Say Nothing at All.
00311105 Easy Piano $14.95

MOVIE GREATS – VOLUME 10
And All That Jazz • Chariots of Fire • Come What May • Forrest Gump • I Finally Found Someone • Iris • Mission: Impossible Theme • Tears in Heaven • There You'll Be • A Wink and a Smile.
00311106 Easy Piano $14.95

DISNEY BLOCKBUSTERS – VOLUME 11
Be Our Guest • Can You Feel the Love Tonight • Go the Distance • Look Through My Eyes • Reflection • Two Worlds • Under the Sea • A Whole New World • Written in the Stars • You've Got a Friend in Me.
00311107 Easy Piano $14.95

CHRISTMAS FAVORITES – VOLUME 12
Blue Christmas • Frosty the Snow Man • Here Comes Santa Claus • I'll Be Home for Christmas • Silver Bells • Wonderful Christmastime • and more.
00311257 Easy Piano $14.95

CHILDREN'S SONGS – VOLUME 13
Any Dream Will Do • Do-Re-Mi • It's a Small World • Linus and Lucy • The Rainbow Connection • Splish Splash • This Land Is Your Land • Winnie the Pooh • Yellow Submarine • Zip-A-Dee-Doo-Dah.
00311258 Easy Piano $14.95

CHILDREN'S FAVORITES – VOLUME 14
Alphabet Song • Frere Jacques • Home on the Range • My Bonnie Lies over the Ocean • Oh! Susanna • Old MacDonald • This Old Man • Yankee Doodle • and more.
00311259 Easy Piano $14.95

DISNEY'S BEST – VOLUME 15
Beauty and the Beast • Bibbidi-Bobbidi-Boo • Chim Chim Cher-ee • Colors of the Wind • Friend Like Me • Hakuna Matata • Part of Your World • Someday • When She Loved Me • You'll Be in My Heart.
00311260 Easy Piano $14.95

LENNON & McCARTNEY HITS – VOLUME 16
Eleanor Rigby • Hey Jude • The Long and Winding Road • Love Me Do • Lucy in the Sky with Diamonds • Nowhere Man • Please Please Me • Sgt. Pepper's Lonely Hearts Club Band • Strawberry Fields Forever • Yesterday.
00311262 Easy Piano $14.95

HOLIDAY HITS – VOLUME 17
Christmas Time Is Here • Feliz Navidad • I Saw Mommy Kissing Santa Claus • Jingle-Bell Rock • The Most Wonderful Time of the Year • My Favorite Things • Santa Claus Is Comin' to Town • and more.
00311329 Easy Piano $14.95

HIGH SCHOOL MUSICAL – VOLUME 18
Bop to the Top • Breaking Free • Get'cha Head in the Game • Stick to the Status Quo • We're All in This Together • What I've Been Looking For • When There Was Me and You • and more.
00311752 Easy Piano $14.95

HIGH SCHOOL MUSICAL 2 – VOLUME 19
All for One • Everyday • Fabulous • Gotta Go My Own Way • I Don't Dance • What Time Is It • Work This Out • You Are the Music in Me.
00311753 Easy Piano $14.99

ANDREW LLOYD WEBBER – FAVORITES – VOLUME 20
Another Suitcase in Another Hall • Any Dream Will Do • As If We Never Said Goodbye • I Believe My Heart • Memory • Think of Me • Unexpected Song • Whistle down the Wind • You Must Love Me • and more.
00311775 Easy Piano $14.99

GREAT CLASSICAL MELODIES – VOLUME 21
Arioso • Ave Maria • Fur Elise • Jesu, Joy of Man's Desiring • Lullaby (Cradle Song) • Meditation • Ode to Joy • Romeo and Juliet (Love Theme) • Sicilienne • Theme from Swan Lake • and more.
00311776 Easy Piano $14.99

ANDREW LLOYD WEBBER – HITS – VOLUME 22
Don't Cry for Me Argentina • I Don't Know How to Love Him • Love Changes Everything • The Music of the Night • No Matter What • Wishing You Were Somehow Here Again • With One Look • and more.
00311785 Easy Piano $14.95

Prices, contents and availability subject to change without notice.

FOR MORE INFORMATION, SEE YOUR LOCAL MUSIC DEALER,
OR WRITE TO:

7777 W. BLUEMOUND RD. P.O.BOX 13819 MILWAUKEE, WI 53213

www.halleonard.com

0109